TIME

Lesley Newson

Contents

SCIENCE MYSTERIES

A&C BLACK · LONDON

Telling the time

Human beings have many ways of telling the time. We can give every moment its own time address, a label of words and numbers that tells us when something happened or is due to happen. If your school term starts on September 5th at 8.30 am you know when to be there. We can measure to a hundredth of a second the time it takes for a runner to win a race. We can scan ancient fossil bones to find out how many years ago an extinct animal walked the Earth. We can even look at the stars and estimate how long ago the Universe began.

Today's runners can compete without even appearing on the same track. They work out who's best by comparing the time it takes them to run a given distance.

Yet time is still a mystery. Knowing how to 'tell the time' isn't the same as understanding it. Telling the time is something we invented to make life easier to organise. Time itself is **not** a human invention. It's something that seems to have started long before humans existed and it will go on long after we have become extinct.

We were all taught about time when we were young but learning to read a clock isn't the same as understanding time.

2

Do you ever get annoyed at the the way modern life seems to depend on the clock?

The Universe has time just like it has space. The difference is that we can travel around in space. Time seems to carry us along with it, always in the same direction, always at the same speed. When we travel along a road, we can see what lies ahead and look back at where we've been. That's not true with time. Some people claim to know the future and everyone can remember and learn about times past, but the only time we can really see is the time we call *now*.

Was there really such a thing as the beginning of time and, if so, when did it happen? Can time go backwards? Will it ever be possible to invent a time machine?

SEIKO

Scientists and philosophers have been thinking about questions like these since prehistoric times. Slowly their understanding has increased. They have learned about how humans and other animals experience time. They have discovered that the bodies of living things have their own ways of telling time. And they are beginning to find out about the nature of time itself. Some of the things they have found out are strange and may be almost impossible for the human mind to accept but if you're interested in time, this is an exciting time to be alive.

Time and life

If you are like most people, you live your life according to a timetable. On a school day, you get up, get ready, go to school, go home, perhaps watch some television, do some homework and go to bed. Being able to tell the time gets you to school before the bell rings and lets you know when your favourite television programmes are on. But it isn't the clock on your wrist that tells you to feel hungry at mealtimes or sleepy at bedtime.

The clock on your wrist tells you when it's time to go to school, but there also seems to be a clock inside you that tells you when it's getting near lunchtime.

Time and temperature

There is a clock inside the human body that makes it work according to a daily pattern. Scientists can show part of this pattern by measuring body temperature throughout the day. Even though we don't feel warmer or colder, our body temperature rises and falls by about half a degree each day. Our bodies are coldest in the middle of the night and then, as waking up time approaches, we begin to warm up. At the end of the day, our bodies start to become cooler, ready for sleep.

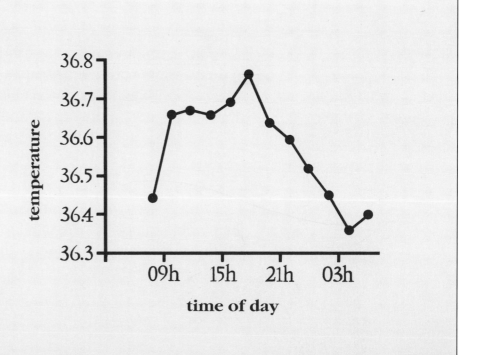

Scientists have found that the levels of certain chemicals in the body, called hormones, rise and fall according to a daily pattern. Hormones travel in the blood and act as signals to cells and organs. The changing level of hormones is linked to changes in the way the body works. During the day, most people need to go to the toilet several times, but most of us go the whole night without having to get up to go to the toilet. That's because, at night, the brain releases chemical signals to the kidneys instructing them to remove less water from the blood. This means that the body makes more concentrated urine but less of it, so the person won't need to go to the toilet for several hours.

We also go all night without eating. Few people go without food for eight or more hours during the day. Your liver contains a store of food and during the night it slowly releases these stored food chemicals into your blood, so you don't wake up (in the middle of the night) feeling hungry.

Scientists have sophisticated techniques for detecting many different chemicals in the blood and body tissues. They have found that the concentrations of many important chemicals are different at different times of the day.

Most people feel sleepiest at night. Scientists have tested people's mental and physical ability at various times of the day and night. They have discovered that people perform best when their bodies are warmest and worst in the middle of the night when they are coldest. Other mammals show a similar pattern of changes throughout the day, except that they happen in reverse in animals such as hamsters and bats which are active during the night and asleep during the day.

Scientists believe that the body's timetable of changes is controlled by a tiny living clock which is found in the brains of all mammals. This cluster of cells, about the size of a pinhead, is called the 'supra-chiasmatic nucleus'. It forms part of the 'hypothalamus', which is the gland that sends signals to the kidneys, liver and other parts of the body. It does this by releasing chemicals which travel around in the blood. Chemical signals from the hypothalamus also set the body's temperature and control the levels of many important body chemicals.

In one very important way, the tiny clock inside your brain is quite different from the kind of clock on the wall or the watch on your wrist. As long as its batteries are working or it's kept wound up, a watch will keep ticking away the seconds and minutes. Experiments have shown that the body's clock is cleverer than this – it resets itself every day. A cable of nerves runs from your eyes to your supra-chiasmatic nucleus carrying information about how light it is. The bright light of dawn lets the bundle of cells know that the day is beginning.

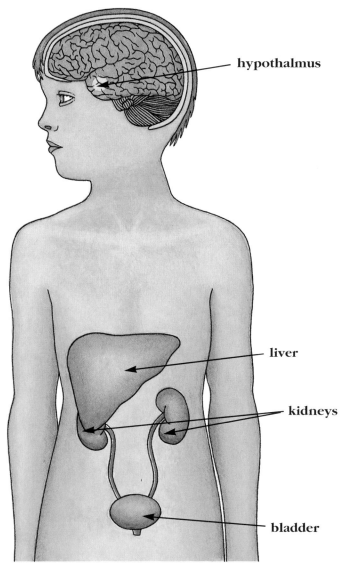

hypothalmus

liver

kidneys

bladder

Most of the scientists who study body rhythms believe that the supra-chiasmatic nucleus is only one of the means that animal bodies have of keeping time. Many animals also follow a yearly timetable. Those living in parts of the world that have a winter season begin to prepare for it long before the cold weather arrives. Some store food. Many grow a warmer coat. They may build a nest to hibernate in, or they may migrate to warmer parts of the world.

Many animals behave differently at different times of the year. These geese know when it's time to migrate.

As winter ends, the animals prepare to make the most of the warm months to come. They lose their winter coats. They mate and start building nests where they can bring up their young.

As well as going through daily changes, animals' bodies follow a yearly timetable which equips them to survive in different seasons.

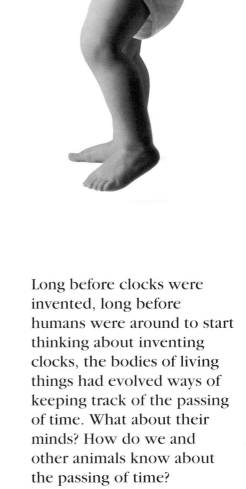

The bodies of animals also follow a timetable that controls their growth and development. The human body is no exception. All human babies begin to sit up, walk, talk and grow teeth at a set time of their life. When children reach a certain age, they begin turning into adults with bodies that allow them to become parents. After that, females begin to release an egg about every four weeks. The body keeps changing as it grows older and, in time, it becomes frail and dies. Your body is following a life plan that depends on it knowing how old you are.

Just like other animals, the human body and mind are programmed to go through different stages at set times in our growing up.

1 month	**Lifts up his head and moves it to keep a moving object in sight**
3 months	**Reaches out for toys and holds on to them briefly**
6 months	**Picks things up and drops them on purpose**
9 months	**Feeds himself with fingers or spoon**
12 months	**Stands up and walks around holding on to furniture**

Long before clocks were invented, long before humans were around to start thinking about inventing clocks, the bodies of living things had evolved ways of keeping track of the passing of time. What about their minds? How do we and other animals know about the passing of time?

The time instinct

Try to imagine a world in which nothing happens, nothing changes. In a world like this, there would be no time. But our world, our Universe, is changing all the time. Lots is happening.

If you think about it, there are three kinds of happening: things that are happening now, things that have already happened, and things that haven't happened yet. This seems so obvious many people might think it is silly to even talk about it. But why do we find it so obvious? We seem to have some sort of instinct that tells us how things are ordered in time.

A squirrel with perfect timing

Many people leave peanuts out to feed the blue tits only to find that they've been snatched by a clever squirrel. This squirrel is about to achieve its goal, after proving that it can negotiate an extraordinary number of different obstacles. This shows that humans are not the only animals that can solve problems. In order to work out and remember the complicated series of tasks it had to perform to get to the top of the pole, this squirrel must have the same sort of intinctive understanding of time that we possess.

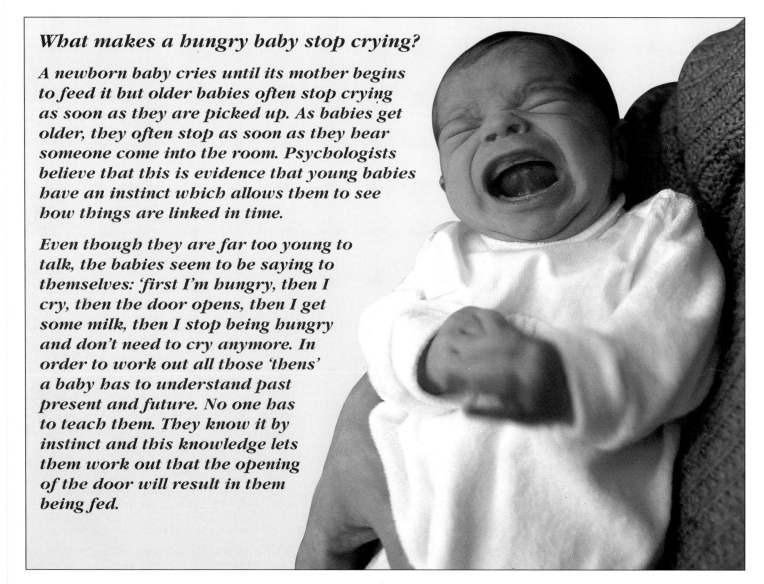

What makes a hungry baby stop crying?

A newborn baby cries until its mother begins to feed it but older babies often stop crying as soon as they are picked up. As babies get older, they often stop as soon as they hear someone come into the room. Psychologists believe that this is evidence that young babies have an instinct which allows them to see how things are linked in time.

Even though they are far too young to talk, the babies seem to be saying to themselves: 'first I'm hungry, then I cry, then the door opens, then I get some milk, then I stop being hungry and don't need to cry anymore. In order to work out all those 'thens' a baby has to understand past present and future. No one has to teach them. They know it by instinct and this knowledge lets them work out that the opening of the door will result in them being fed.

This time instinct is not something special that only humans have. When a dog sees its owner open the cupboard and get out the lead, it gets excited. It has worked out that 'my owner gets out my lead, then we go out for a walk'. All but the simplest animals have the brainpower to know that some happenings follow other happenings and remember the links between them. Without this inbuilt knowledge, it would be impossible for living things to learn.

We also seem to have an instinctive ability to 'keep time'. Even people who can't read music or follow a tune can enjoy beating out a rhythm and do it extremely accurately. We enjoy music that has a beat and like to make our bodies follow the rhythm. Even young children like to dance and make rhythmic noises. It's something we are born with. Again, humans are not special in this. A dog wags its tail in a rhythmic way. Many horses pass the time by rhythmically swaying or pawing the ground.

Keeping time seems to be something that is programmed into our brains. Why do we like music with a beat and get pleasure out of moving our body to a rhythm?

Scientists believe that an animal's ability to 'keep time' gives us clues to how the brain works. In order to have control of the body, the brain must do an enormous number of things and get its timing absolutely right. A simple action like scratching your nose is amazingly complicated.

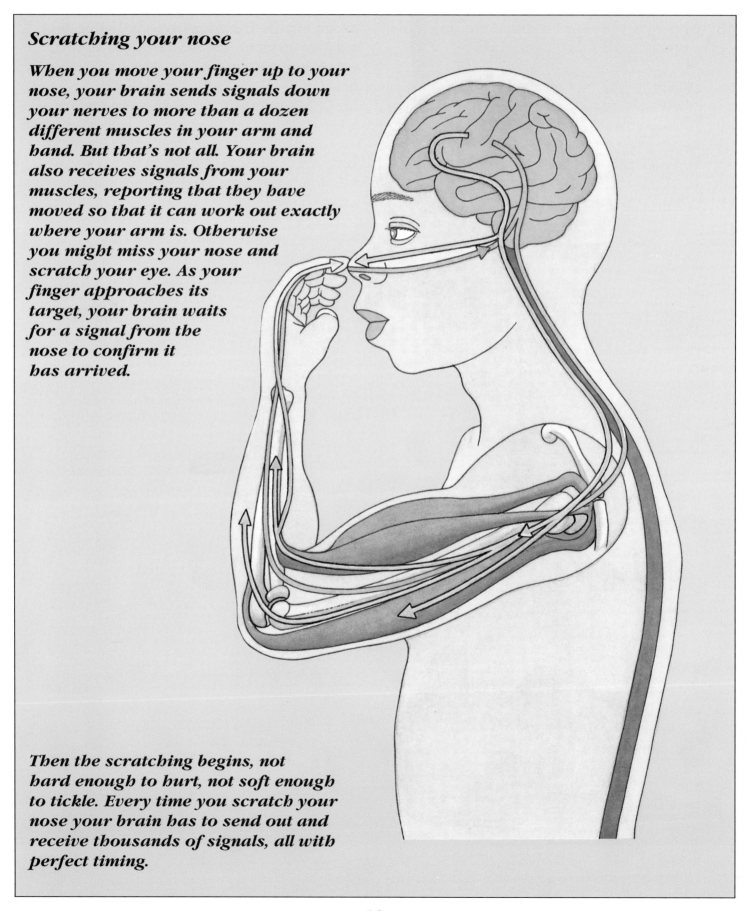

Scratching your nose

When you move your finger up to your nose, your brain sends signals down your nerves to more than a dozen different muscles in your arm and hand. But that's not all. Your brain also receives signals from your muscles, reporting that they have moved so that it can work out exactly where your arm is. Otherwise you might miss your nose and scratch your eye. As your finger approaches its target, your brain waits for a signal from the nose to confirm it has arrived.

Then the scratching begins, not hard enough to hurt, not soft enough to tickle. Every time you scratch your nose your brain has to send out and receive thousands of signals, all with perfect timing.

Your brain and the brains of other complicated animals can only work this well by keeping many things in mind at once. And it doesn't just have to keep in mind things that are happening right now. It also has to keep in mind things that have just happened. For your brain to do its job, 'now' has to last for longer than an instant.

You can see this by looking at the way your brain works when it does certain quite ordinary things. Have you noticed that, if a friend tells you his telephone number, you can repeat it back to him straight away? Your brain is able to keep all those numbers in mind, but only for a short while. A few seconds later, they've gone.

Tests on humans have shown that our brains usually keep things in mind for just under a second, but this can stretch to a second and a half. Thoughts that make sense, like a series of words seem to be kept for a longer time. A favourite trick of teachers is to ask a question and then suddenly say the name of a student who is obviously not paying attention.

Annoyingly for the teacher, the student is often able to give a sensible answer to the question. This is possible because the daydreaming student's brain had stored the teacher's question without the student even realising it.

Many of the things you do are done to a beat that may be fast or slow but is always within the time that your brain keeps things in mind. There is a rhythm to the movement of your legs when you walk or run, of your fingers when you scratch, of your mouth when you chew and of your arm when you use a tool like a hammer or a toothbrush. You can change the timing of the rhythm, but if you try to do things too quickly or slowly your movements become uncoordinated.

So it seems that we and many other animals are born with a body and brain that know about time and live according to it. But that is not the same as understanding time.

In tennis as in all sports, timing is essential. The body must remember exactly what to do and when if the ball is to hit the racket at just the right moment.

Back in the mists of time

Human beings seem to be the only animal that wants to understand things just because they find them interesting. No one knows when people first started trying to understand time, but 50,000 years ago a group of people living in southern France were probably thinking about time when they created this piece of bone engraved with 69 tiny marks.

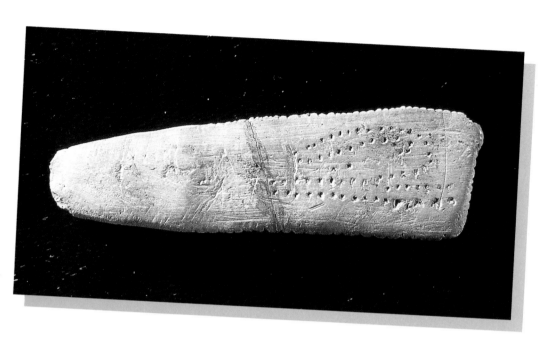

In the early 1900s, archaeologists found the bone near the French town of Blanchard. Pieces of bone with similar engravings on them have been found buried among the remains of many ancient dwellings in other parts of Europe and Africa. The people who made them were Stone Age people and they had no metal tools. The engravings had been painstakingly made with a sharp flint point. What were these pieces of bone for?

The meaning of the marks remained a mystery until the 1960s, when a science writer named Alexander Marshack suggested an answer. He followed the series of marks in the curving line and saw that they show the way the Moon seems to grow from a thin crescent to a circle, shrink back to a crescent and begin to grow again. Marshack believes that the bone helped people to keep track of time.

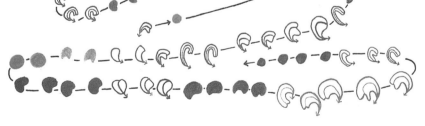

The changing shape of the Moon provided our ancestors with a way of noting the passing months.

The people who made the marks on the piece of bone couldn't read, write words or do arithmetic. Clocks hadn't been invented then, of course, and neither had the system of numbers which we use to give each day a date. But that doesn't mean these people were stupid. The tools and works of art they left behind showed that they lived a complicated life and needed a way of keeping track of time.

They could work out the time of day by the position of the Sun in the sky, but they also needed to keep track of the days, months and seasons. For this, the Moon would have been more useful, especially with the help of a record of how the Moon changes. The 69 marks on the bone show the Moon's changes over two and a half months, about the length of a season. It was much colder in Europe during the Stone Age, and 69 days may have been the usual length of the winter, from the first frost to the melting of the rivers.

If different families or tribes had arranged the year before to meet at a certain place in a certain season in order to have a feast, to exchange gifts or seek a husband or wife, they would be able to look at the sky, consult their record of the way the Moon would change and then be able to judge when they would all get together.

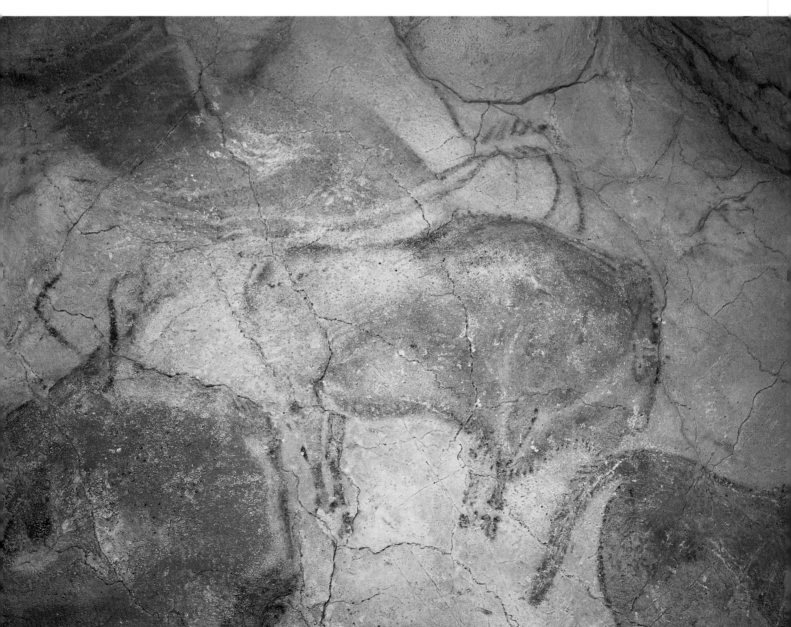

This cave painting of bison was created by people living more than 15,000 years ago. These people weren't savages. They may not have had computers and videos but they lived complex lives and had to keep track of time.

About four thousand years ago, the people of Northern Europe invented another way of keeping track of the changing seasons. They were farmers and needed to know when spring would arrive so they could plant their crops at the best time. The calendars they invented and built can still be seen. The most spectacular is called Stonehenge, but around 600 simpler stone circle calendars have been found in other parts of Britain, Europe and North America.

The stone circles remained long after the farms were destroyed and for thousands of years no one could imagine why these rings of stones had been made. In the middle of the 20th Century, archaeologists studying Stonehenge realised that the circles could be used to make quite precise observations of the Sun, Moon and stars.

Stonehenge may have been a place of worship but it also had a down-to-earth use, as a device for telling the time.

Each morning, the Sun rises at a point on the horizon which is slightly different to the day before. In the coldest part of the year, the sunrise happens further to the south. As the days become warmer, the point moves north. The ancient farmers must have noticed this, because the stones in their giant calendars are carefully positioned to help them keep track of the Sun's rising place. The points on the horizon could be picked out by lining up two stones. Once the position of the sunrise reached a certain point, the farmers knew spring had really arrived and it was time to plant their crops.

For thousands of years, human beings told the time by looking at the sky. Many of the units we use to divide up time are based on the things they saw. A day is the time from sunrise to sunrise. We now know that this is the time it takes for the Earth to make one rotation. A month is the approximate time it takes for the Moon to change through all its phases. We now know that this is the time (about 29 and a half days) it takes for the Moon to orbit the Earth. A year is the time it takes for the Sun to return to the same sunrise position. We now know that this is the time (about 365 and a quarter days) it takes for the Earth to orbit the Sun.

Because our ancient ancestors measured time by looking at changes in the Earth and sky, they looked upon time as travelling in a circle. The Sun rose, set and then rose again. The Moon grew, shrank, disappeared and grew again. Living things began growing in the spring, died back in the winter and grew again. Looking at time in this way probably meant that our ancient ancestors never thought of time as having a beginning or an end. Time just went round and round. In many cultures, people believed that their own lives travelled in a circle. They believed that after they died they would be re-born as new babies.

Each day of the year, the Sun rises in a slightly different place on the horizon.

In nature, time seems to travel in a circle, a series of deaths and re-births. Some cultures believe human life also goes in a circle.

Today, most people see time as travelling in a straight line rather than a circle. We still see nature go through the seasonal changes that happen in the same way each year but we also see our world changing in ways that are permanent. People are trying to change the world for the better and fear that it is getting worse. Few of us believe we are part of a never-ending cycle of change.

This change in the way we view time may have begun when our ancestors invented a system of counting and numbering things. They soon started to number their days and years. Numbers don't form a circle that repeats periodically. They are on a line that stretches forever in both directions. For us, the minutes, days and years seem to do the same thing.

A Universe of laws

Once our ancestors became more adept at working with numbers, they were able to learn about the world in a new way. They could do experiments, take measurements and use mathematics to describe the way things behave in our world. For many years though, our ancestors had no good way of measuring time. They could get an idea of the time of day by looking at the position of the Sun or they could keep track of periods of time with sand or water clocks but this wasn't the same as measuring time.

The discovery that lead to the invention of a mechanical clock was made in the 16th Century by the Italian scientist Galileo Galilei. One day, when he was attending a service in the cathedral at Pisa, he watched the swinging of a big chandelier that hung from the ceiling. Then he noticed that each swing of the chandelier took the same amount of time. Sometimes it made big swings quickly; sometimes it made small swings slowly but it always took the same time to travel from one side to the other.

Galileo (1564-1642) was one of the first people to notice that things seemed to move according to natural laws.

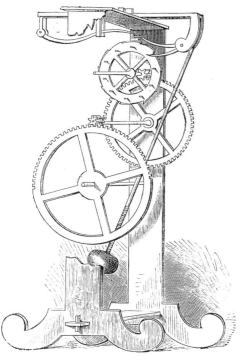

This is a drawing of the mechanical clock which Galileo designed but never got around to building.

Many years later, Galileo did some experiments to learn more about how a hanging weight or 'pendulum' swings. He found that the size and weight of the pendulum doesn't affect the time it takes to make its swing. The time depends only on the length of the string that the weight is hanging on. Galileo went on to work out how a swinging pendulum could be attached to a mechanical device for clocking up passing seconds, minutes and hours. Fifteen years after Galileo's death a Dutch scientist called Christiaan Huygens succeeded in using his ideas to make the first working pendulum clock.

During his life Galileo made observations about the way many things move, not just pendulums. He studied the movement of objects in space that he could see with a telescope, and objects on Earth that fell to the ground with ever increasing speed. He realised that movement is linked with time. You measure speed, for example, by knowing the time it takes to travel a certain distance. But can you understand movement without understanding time?

Towards the end of the 17th Century, the English scientist Isaac Newton, began to study the way things move. He found that objects move in a predictable way as though their movements are governed by some sort of natural laws. In 1687 he published a book explaining his ideas about these 'Laws of Motion', and describing how 'forces' work to change the speed and direction of moving objects. He also described 'gravity' as a force that pulls objects towards one another. The scientists of the day immediately recognised that Newton had discovered something very important. Today, most children learn about Newton's ideas of forces, movement and gravity when they are in primary school.

Newton (1642-1727) worked out the laws which physical objects seem to follow as they move.

Newton believed in an 'absolute time' which governed movements and change, not just on Earth but everywhere in the Universe.

Like Galileo, Newton knew that understanding movement had to be linked with understanding time but here he had a problem. He could learn about movement by watching the way things moved, but Newton could think of no way to observe the behaviour of time. So, in working out his ideas about movement, Newton decided to follow his *feelings* about the nature of time. He knew that people often sense time travelling at different speeds; sometimes it rushes by and sometimes it drags. He knew that the clocks which had just been invented often ran fast or slow. But Newton believed there had to be an 'absolute time' which ran at the same speed everywhere in the Universe. For him, time seemed to be part of the Universe, just like space, matter and energy.

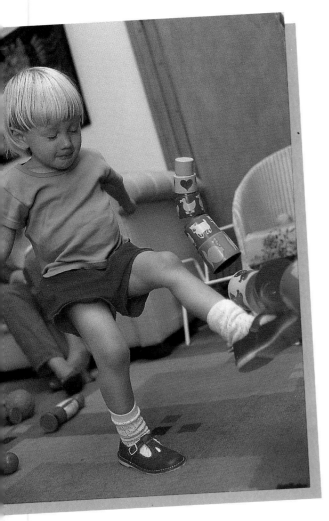

Newton's era and the centuries that followed it have been a period of great scientific discovery. People have learned more about the nature of the Earth and Universe in the last 400 years than their ancestors had managed to find out in thousands of years. But discovering the nature of time was not easy. Most scientists just went along with Newton's idea of there being an 'absolute time' that constantly travelled at the same speed and in the same direction.

What do people mean when they say time travels in one direction? We can only experience time going forward but we can *watch* it running backwards by making a video tape play backwards. This allows us to see the kinds of impossible things that would happen if time ran backwards. For example, we might see a puddle of milk and some pieces of glass slurp off the floor, leap into the air and reorganise themselves into a glass of milk on a table. In our Universe this sort of thing just doesn't happen.

During the 19th Century, scientists began to look carefully at the sorts of things that do and don't happen in our Universe. In simple terms, they concluded that the things that happen without effort are things which make the Universe more disorganised. In our Universe, things never spontaneously become more organised. Time travels in the direction of greater disorganisation.

It takes work to organise things but creating chaos is easy. This seems to be something everyone learns, and enjoys learning, when they are very young.

The universal untidiness law

Anyone who is supposed to keep his or her bedroom tidy will agree that there must be some sort of universal law that drives things in the direction of greater disorganisation. Rooms seem to become untidy by themselves but tidying them up takes energy. Your body gets its energy from food. As it digests food to extract energy from it, the chemicals that make up your food are broken up into less organised chemicals.

Food is a fuel for us because it contains many chemicals that are highly organised and building these organised chemicals takes energy. In the case of the vegetables and other plant food we eat, that energy comes from the Sun. Plants use energy from the Sun to build their organised chemicals from simple chemicals like water and carbon dioxide. The energy from the Sun is created when matter in the middle of th Sun turns into heat and light. As this happens, the Sun becomes more disorganised.

So, no matter what we and other living things do to try and get organised, the Universe as a whole is always becoming more disorganised.

Spilling milk never organises itself back into the glass. This would only be possible if time ran backwards.

The understanding that time travels in one direction, towards more disorganisation, led many 19th century scientists to reach a rather dismal conclusion: time will eventually run out. The Universe is doomed. Sometime in the future, it will become as disorganised as it possibly can. Then there will be no more energy, no more changes and no more time.

So is that all there is to time and the Universe? This is the way it looked to many scientists about a hundred years ago. But as they did more research, scientists began to discover that the Universe is a much bigger and much stranger place than anyone had ever imagined.

Stretching and warping

As the end of the 19th Century approached, scientists were feeling rather smug about how well they understood the Universe. They knew about gravity, light, electricity, magnetism. . . the list went on and on. Some thought they might soon understand everything. Few suspected that early in the 20th Century they'd have to change their minds about almost everything, even time.

The problems started with investigations into light. In 1865, James Clerk Maxwell showed that light, radio waves and other kinds of radiation have to travel at fixed speed. But how is this speed is fixed? Light travels at a fixed speed compared to what?

James Clerk Maxwell (1831-1879) was a brilliant mathematician and used his skills to understand more about how electricity, magnetism and light behave.

We don't usually think about it but whenever we measure the speed of something that moves, we always measure its speed compared to something else. For example, a train going at 50 miles an hour is travelling at 50 miles an hour compared to the railway line. But imagine that there are two trains travelling on lines that running side by side. If the two trains are traveling at 50 miles an hour in opposite directions, then one is going at 100 miles per hour compared to the other.

Light moves so quickly it's impossible to imagine a beam of light travelling along, but the scientists tried. Light from the Sun travels through space and the scientists thought there had to be something in space for light to travel through. They called this something 'ether' and decided that light must travel at a fixed speed compared to the ether. In 1887, two scientists called Albert Michelson and Edward Morley decided to do an experiment based on this idea.

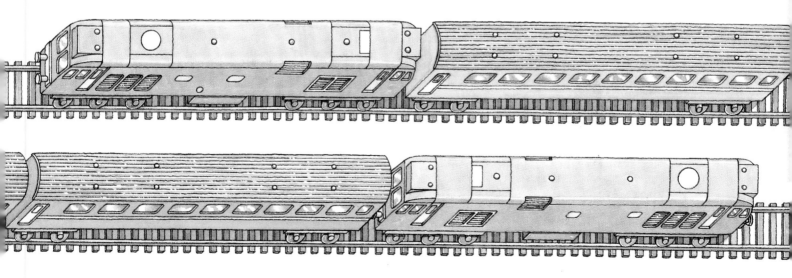

Michelson and Morley's experiment

What Michelson and Morley were really trying to do was measure the speed of the Earth as it orbits the Sun. They had worked out a way of doing this using two beams of light. One beam shone in the same direction as the movement of the Earth as it orbits the Sun. The other shone at right angles to the Earth's movement.

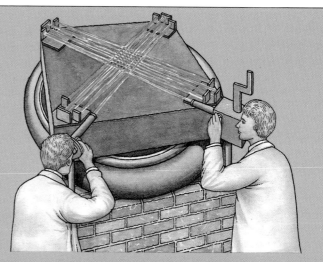

The beam of light travelling in the same direction as the Earth would, they thought, get to the detector first because it would travel at the speed of light plus the speed of the Earth. The other beam would be slower because it would only travel at the speed of light. They planned to calculate the speed of the Earth by subtracting one from the other. It seemed simple but when they did the experiment they got a shock. No matter how many times they made the measurement they found that both beams of light reached the detector at exactly the same time.

Albert Einstein (1879-1955) was only 25 when he wrote his famous scientific paper which revolutionised the way scientists think about the Universe.

Michelson and Morley's experiment showed that there was something wrong with scientists' ideas about light. The beams of light always seemed to travel at the same speed. This didn't fit it with the rest of what scientists believed about the workings of the Universe. In 1905, a young clerk who worked in the patent office in Switzerland published a paper which showed how these results could make sense, but only if scientists changed a lot of their ideas. The clerk's name was Albert Einstein.

Einstein said that there is no such thing as ether. Light doesn't travel at a certain speed compared to anything else. It simply always travels at the same speed and everyone measuring the speed of light will always get the same result, no matter how they themselves are moving.

Assuming the speed of light to be constant, Einstein worked out a new theory of the way the Universe behaves. He used mathematics to look again at the movement of objects. Scientists had believed for over 200 years that Newton's calculations gave a perfect description of how objects move in our Universe. Einstein's calculations showed the Universe behaving in a slightly different way. One thing they showed is that Newton's idea of the Universe having an unchanging 'absolute time' can't be true.

Einstein pointed out that, if the speed of light remains constant then time can't be constant. For example, the time it takes for a beam of light to travel a distance, will seem different for people travelling at different speeds but according to Einstein, this isn't because **light** is travelling at different speeds but because **time** travels at different speeds depending on the speed of the observer. This seems impossible but many experiments have been done to test Einstein's theory and all of them have confirmed that going fast stretches time in exactly the way the theory predicts.

In one set of experiments, scientists put extremely accurate atomic clocks in a high speed aeroplane and compared the time they measured with identical clocks on the ground. The clocks in the plane ran a tiny bit slower than those on the ground. At low speeds the difference is small but Einstein's equations predict that time gets more stretched as speeds get closer to the speed of light. Since light travels at 300,000 kilometres per second (186,000 miles per second), it isn't surprising we don't notice time stretching during a 70 mile per hour car journey or even in a jumbo jet which flies at a mere 550 miles per hour.

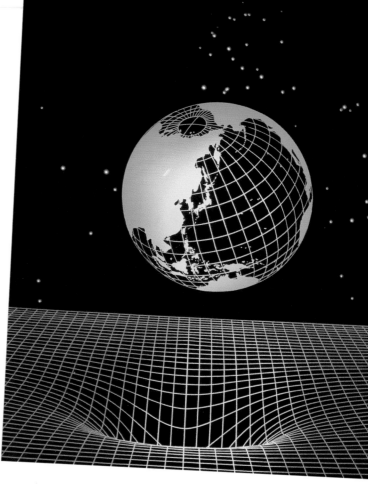

Artists have created pictures to try to help people grasp the idea of gravity being a warp in Spacetime. In this one, the orange grid represents the invisible 'fabric of Spacetime' which is being warped by the mass of the Earth.

By 1915, Einstein had worked out how gravity operates in a Universe where light has one speed and time stretches. Newton's ideas of space and time may describe the workings of the Universe reasonably well but Einstein's mathematics showed that it is more accurate to think of the Universe as having four dimentional 'Spacetime'. His calculations also suggested that what we call 'gravity' is not a 'force', as Newton believed, but a curve or 'warp' in Spacetime.

According to Einstein, a massive object in space like the Earth warps Spacetime in a way that makes matter curve toward its centre. This may seem like a pulling force but it's quite different. The warping of Spacetime doesn't just affect matter. A beam of light should also seem to curve as it goes past a massive object. And, being near a massive object should change the speed of time.

Einstein used mathematics to work out his ideas and people can only fully understand the ideas if they can follow this mathematics.

It sounds bizarre but, again, experiment after experiment has shown that Einstein was absolutely right. Astronomers now take for granted that light travelling from distant stars curves as it passes massive objects in space. Engineers who design satellite navigation systems always take into account the fact that time travels faster at the satellite than it does on the surface of the Earth. The satellite is further away from the centre of the Earth so its Spacetime is not as warped as ours.

This picture, taken with the Hubble Space Telescope, is visible proof that Einstein was right about massive objects warping Spacetime. The bright spot in the centre is a massive object, a galaxy which is relatively close to our galaxy. The four spots around it are a single very distant and very bright object called a quasar. We see four spots rather than one because the mass of the galaxy has warped Spacetime making the light from the quasar bend so that it travels in four slightly different directions.

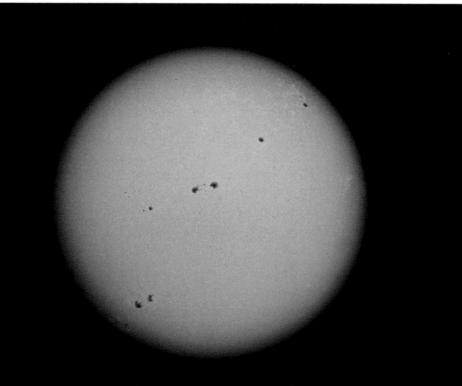

Einstein showed that matter can be turned into energy and this explained the source of the Sun's energy. The crushing gravity in the centre of stars squeezes hydrogen atoms into helium atoms and turns a small amount of the matter into energy.

The only way to understand Einstein's ideas fully is to look at the mathematics he used. He described the Universe mathematically and other physicists saw his descriptions made sense by following the series of equations he wrote as he worked out his ideas.

Einstein's most important equation is so well known that many people have heard of it even if they don't understand it. It is $[E = mc^2]$. (Where E stands for energy, m stands for the mass of matter, and c stands for the speed of light.) This equation shows how, under the right conditions, a very small amount of matter can turn into a very large amount of energy. This is how energy is produced in the centre of stars, in a nuclear power station and in a nuclear bomb.

In the beginning

Einstein's calculations showed the Universe to be quite different from the way people had imagined it, and even Einstein himself was puzzled about one of his ideas. He believed that the Universe stays as it is, but if his calculations about gravity were correct, the stars and the energy they release should be causing huge warps in Spacetime. Why didn't the Universe collapse or fly apart? The answer to this puzzle came when scientists learned more about stars, and revealed even more unexpected facts about the Universe and time.

In 1924, an astronomer named Edwin Hubble announced a discovery that astonished everyone. He'd been studying some very faint stars and worked out that they weren't ordinary dim stars. They were very bright stars that only looked faint because they were incredibly far away, much further away than than the most distant stars in our Galaxy. Hubble's discovery showed that our Milky Way is not the only galaxy. There are many, many galaxies out there with vast tracts of empty space in between.

Next, Hubble examined the colour of light that shone from the stars in other galaxies. If it was slightly different from the colour of stars in our Galaxy, it would show that the other galaxies are moving around in space compared to ours. To his surprise, Hubble saw that the light from all the galaxies looked red. What's more, the more distant the galaxy, the redder it looked. This happens because all the galaxies are moving away from us and from each other. The space between the galaxies is increasing all the time.

This solved Einstein's puzzle. He didn't need to explain why the Universe stays as it is because it doesn't stay as it is. It's expanding.

This is the faint glow of the most distant galaxy yet discovered, as detected by the Hubble Space Telescope. Scientists believe the light left the galaxy up to 14 billion years ago, when the Universe was very young.

What does all this have to do with time? Well, if the Universe is getting bigger, then it used to be smaller. The further back in time you go, the smaller it becomes. If you go far enough back in time do you find its beginning? That's what it seemed like.

As a result of Hubble's discoveries, a new scientific specialism began called 'cosmology', the study of the cosmos. Some cosmologists calculated that billions of years ago there was a 'Big Bang' when the Universe exploded into existence. But for others, the idea of time and the Universe having a beginning didn't make sense.

When scientists don't agree, finding new evidence often sorts things out. In 1948, an American cosmologist called George Gamow suggested that space might still be glowing with the energy of its explosive beginning, but that billions of years of expanding and cooling would have reduced the Universe's glow to a low energy form of radiation, called microwaves.

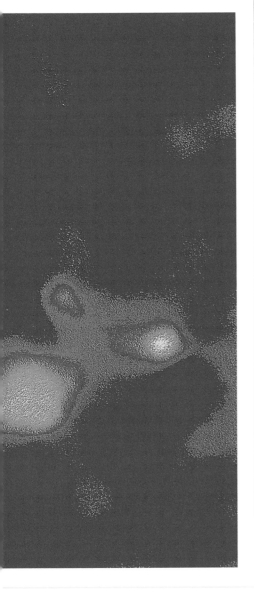

Edwin Hubble (1889-1953) and the telescope he used to discover that there were many other galaxies beyond our own Milky Way Galaxy. Today the Hubble Space Telescope, named after Edwin Hubble, orbits the Earth examining distant galaxies.

Artists struggle to create some kind of image of the Big Bang, what most physicists believe was the first event in the Universe's time.

In 1965, Bob Dicke and Jim Peebles, two physicists at Princeton University were just about to try to detect these microwaves when they heard about a strange discovery made by two physicists at the nearby Bell Telephone Laboratory. Arno Penzias and Robert Wilson were working on a new, very sensitive microwave detector for picking up telephone signals, when they unexpectedly discovered an echo of the Big Bang.

The discovery convinced cosmologists that the Universe and time did have a beginning, but it was still hard to imagine. If you imagined further and further back in time with the Universe getting smaller and smaller, what do find at the beginning of time? The whole Universe shrunk to nothing?

In 1965, a British physicist called Stephen Hawking read a scientific paper written by another Briton, Roger Penrose and began to form an idea about what that 'nothing', could be.

Penrose's paper was actually about what happens to old stars. Gravity makes stars shine by squeezing together hydrogen atoms until they fuse. The energy released by this fusion travels outwards. Penrose wanted to find out what happens to stars once all their hydrogen fuel is used up and the explosions stop. He used Einstein's calculations about how gravity warps Spacetime, and found that old stars literally collapse under their own weight.

Stephen Hawking worked out that the Big Bang could have begun with something called 'a singularity'.

Penzias and Wilson

Robert Wilson

Arno Penzias

Penzias and Wilson thought there was something wrong with their microwave detector when it kept picking up a mysterious low hiss of microwaves. It seemed to be showing that microwave radiation was coming from every corner of the sky. In fact, they had accidentally discovered a whispering echo of the Big Bang.

An artist has tried to create an image of the way matter from a nearby star spirals down into a black hole. The massive gravity of the black hole tears apart the matter as it approaches releasing a stream of X-rays. A black hole may not shine with light like a star but astronomers believe that the space around them shines with X-rays and this is how they search for black holes.

The larger the star, the denser it becomes and the largest of all undergo a strange transformation. They become infinitely dense points that take up no space at all. Spacetime is so warped at this point that it creates an area from which nothing, not even light, can escape. This area of space became known as a 'black hole' and the strange point at its centre was called a 'singularity'.

A 'singularity', Hawking thought, was also a perfect description of what the Universe must have been in the beginning. Hawking and Penrose met to discuss this idea and to work out the calculations. The conclusion they reached was hard to imagine, but the idea made sense mathematically.

Hawking and Penrose declared that the Universe emerged from a singularity. This isn't a sort of 'cosmic egg' floating around in space that cracks to let out the galaxies. It's much more incredible than that. It's a point that takes up no space but that holds the whole Universe, its time and space as well as its matter and energy.

If Hawking is correct, there was no time, at least not in our Universe, until the Big Bang happened. Like so many of the things predicted by Einstein's equations, 'singularities' and 'black holes' seem unbelievable, but there is strong evidence that they do exist.

This is the core of a nearby galaxy. Some astronomers believe it contains a black hole.

Travelling in time

All this work which is aiming to understand time is interesting in itself, but could there be practical benefits? Will it ever be possible to travel in time?

First of all, travelling to the future is easy. Ordinary life is a trip into the future. By tomorrow, you will have travelled one day forward in time. Einstein's theories show, however, that you don't have to travel to the future at this ordinary speed because time travels more slowly the faster you go.

No one has an idea of how a time machine might work, but there are lots of ideas about how it might look. One of the most famous is Dr Who's Tardis.

If spaceships were invented that could travel about 300,000 times faster than they do today, a group of people could go for a cruise which **they** thought only lasted for a few weeks. But on the slower moving Earth, time would travel much more quickly. Years would have passed. The travellers would return to find their friends and even their children grown old and perhaps dead. Their speedy journey would allow the travellers to live in a future they would never have seen if they had stayed at home. But the travellers would never be able to return home. This kind of time travel can only go in one direction.

Many physicists believe the laws of physics make travel to the past impossible. There are also many common sense reasons for not believing that backward time travel will ever be possible. For example, if people in the future have invented backward time travel, why haven't any of them visited us? Why haven't tourists of the future travelled to 16th-century London to see the first performance of *Romeo and Juliet*?

Shakespeare's Globe Theatre, a holiday destination for tomorrow's time tourist?

28

There are other trickier questions. What if a nosy time tourist was to have a chat with the young William Shakespeare? This might so confuse Shakespeare that he would stop writing. Then future would be changed and the tourist would have had no reason to have made his trip. Even worse, what if this dreadful tourist had taken a copy of the *Complete Works of Shakespeare* back in time and given it to Shakespeare himself as a teenager? Shakespeare would only have to copy out the plays in his own handwriting. This would make the Bard a fraud and leave a big question mark over who actually wrote the plays.

Common sense may suggest that backwards time travel is impossible, but what do the laws of physics say? Einstein's mathematics have shown that gravity is a warp in Spacetime. Could such a warp be so extreme that Spacetime could be torn and folded back on itself? Some physicists believe that these kinds of folds could exist inside a rapidly spinning black hole. Perhaps a black hole could be used to power a journey back in time?

If time travel became possible, would art and history be damaged?

It all sounds fantastic, but as physicists learn more about the Universe and the matter that makes it up, they find themselves questioning more and more of their basic ideas. For example, why do we believe that there is only one Universe? We may only be able to detect one, but there could be many running along in parallel to ours, and branching off into different futures. This would mean that backwards time tourists couldn't interfere with their own future. They wouldn't travel back to the past of their own universe, but to the past of a parallel universe with a different future.

We can't travel to the past but can see into the past. When telescopes such as the Hubble Space Telescope detect light from distant parts of the Universe, they are seeing the Universe as it was because that light left its source billions of years ago.

In the future. . .

How could the Universe with all its matter, energy, laws and time simply burst into being? This is an artist's impression of galaxies forming after the Big Bang.

If cosmologists are correct, however many universes there are, they all had a beginning. Will they all come to an end? Remember that the 19th-century physicists, who didn't know that the Universe is expanding, simply saw the Universe becoming more and more disorganised. Many concluded that time must end when everything becomes completely disorganised and change is no longer possible.

Today's physicists see things differently. Many believe that the Universe has been expanding since it exploded from a singularity several billion years ago, but that the expansion is slowing down. That is because gravity should be acting to pull the matter and energy of the Universe together.

Scientists have carefully studied the hum of radiation leftover from the Big Bang and found that in some parts of space the energy is slightly greater. They believe this is the clue to the structure of the Universe that began to form in the first second of time.

If this is correct three things may happen to the Universe in the future. It could go on expanding forever, gradually slowing down but never coming to a stop. It could slow down so much that it almost stops. Or it could stop expanding but then start shrinking as gravity pulls everything back together again. If this happens, the whole Universe will continue shrinking until everything crushes down to become a singularity again. Time will end just as it began – wrapped in a point of infinite density that takes up no space.

The third possibility is the most interesting. It would mean that the Universe isn't doomed to wind down to a disorganised, changeless and timeless death. Once the movement of the Universe changed direction, its laws of physics might change. Time might run backwards. Everything might start becoming more organised instead of more disorganised. After our Universe collapses into a singularity, there might be another Big Bang and a new universe would be born. It might be the same as our Universe or it might be very different.

It is very hard for the human mind to create a picture of these things. Our minds have become used to believing that time is something that goes on forever at the same speed and in the same direction. Most of us believe we can spend a few pounds in a shop and buy a clock that measures time reliably. It seems incredible that the speed of time itself can be altered by how fast we are moving or by how close we are to the centre of a massive object.

Perhaps our minds are as primitive as those of our prehistoric ancestors who couldn't do arithmetic and couldn't even count. But then, our prehistoric ancestors may have had a truer understanding of the nature of time than we do. If the Universe is destined to shrink and become a singularity again, then it actually is correct to think of time travelling in circles. Just as the Earth has seasons that are repeated year after year, perhaps the Universe has seasons which are billions of years in duration.

The human race has been alive for only a tiny part of the Universe's springtime of expansion. But this tininess shouldn't make us feel unimportant. If the cosmologists are correct, the whole Universe emerged from something so tiny that it took up no space.

Acknowledgements

The author and publisher would like to thank Dr David Jones, University of Newcastle; Prof Roger Taylor, Sussex University; Alexander Marshack, Harvard University.

Photographic credits
Front cover clockwise from bottom right: Chris Fairclough, Chris Fairclough, NASA/ Science Photo Library; Martin Dohrn/Science Photo Library; back cover: (top) Popperfoto, (bottom) Dr Maurice Cross.

page2 (top) Seiko, (bottom) Chris Fairclough Colour Library; page3 (top) Hulton Deutsch Collection, (bottom) Seiko; page4 Bubbles; page5 Science Photo Library; page6 Royal Society for the Protection of Birds; page7 (left) Chris Fairclough Colour Library, (right) Bubbles; page8 Sally and Richard Greenhill; page9 (top) BBC, (bottom) Redferns; page11 Sporting Pictures (UK) Ltd; page12 (both) Alexander Marshack; page13 Giroudon/Bridgeman Art Library; page14 Chris Fairclough Colour Library; page15 (top) Chris Fairclough Colour Library, (bottom) Bridgeman Art Library; page16 (both) Science Photo Library; page17 (top) Bridgeman Art Library, (bottom) Science Photo Library; page18 Sally and Richard Greenhill; page19 Science Photo Library; page20 Science Photo Library; page21 Hulton Deutsch Collection; page22 (top) Science Photo Library, (bottom) Range Pictures; page23 (top) Science Photo Library, (bottom) National Optical Astronomy Observatories; page24 (both) Science Photo Library; page25 Science Photo Library; page26 (left and centre) Science Photo Library; (right) Popperfoto; page27 (both) Science Photo Library; page28 (top) BBC, (bottom) Fotomas Index; page29 (top) Fotomas Index, (bottom) Science Photo Library; page30 (both) Science Photo Library.

First published 1996

A & C Black (Publishers) Limited
35 Bedford Row
London WC1R 4JH

ISBN 0-7136-4025-1

© A & C Black (Publishers) Limited

A CIP catalogue record for this book is available from the British Library.

Illustrations by Jason Lewis

Index